HOROSCOPE 2024 CANCER

Angeline Rubi and Alina A. Rubi

Published Independently

All rights reserved © 2024.

Astrologer: Alina A. Rubi

Editing: Alina. Rubi and Angeline A. Rubi

rubiediciones29@gmail.com

Who is Cancer?

Dates*: June 22nd to July 22nd*

Day*: Monday*

Color*: White, silver*

Element*: Water*

Compatibility*: Taurus, Pisces*

Symbol*:*

Modality*: Cardinal*

Polarity*: Feminine*

Ruling planet*: Moon*

House*: 4*

Metal*: Silver*

Quartz*: Moonstone, pearl, Rose Quartz,*

Constellation*: Cancer*

Cancer Personality

The emotional intelligence of Cancer is incomparable, it is an extremely empathetic sign. They have an acute intuition, that's why they are the most protective of all the zodiac, that's why they are protectors par excellence.

They are always attentive and available to attend to the needs of others, even if that means putting themselves second.

He is emotional and affectionate, and friendly and knows how to be cautious when needed. They like their home and children their home is like a nest, a refuge to go to when stress overwhelms them too much.

They have an excellent memory, especially for personal events and memories of their childhood that they can recall in detail. They live conditioned by their memories of the past and by their imagination of the future.

They are excellent providers and work best when left alone without anyone trying to help them with their work at work.

They treat their jobs the same way they treat their homes. They are protective of their work situation and often hold important positions. They are loyal, expect loyalty and treat their employees like family.

They love to receive endless flattery from others, are ambitious, easily offended and take offense in many situations where there is no reason to do so.

They are very good traders, they like money, to have their savings and that nobody knows how much they have. They are a little distrustful when it comes to starting a love relationship, they give a lot of thought to this situation because they are afraid of getting hurt, so they do not get carried away by their feelings or passions, as they must first make sure they are with the right person to gamble everything for everything, because they give their feelings, trust and love without reservation.

They are very detailed and romantic, when they have a partner, they do not allow anyone to get in the way of their relationship, not even to give them advice on how to manage it or what is best at any given moment.

General Cancer Horoscope

This is a fabulous year for new beginnings, new businesses, and projects. What you start now will be the focus for the next 5 years of your life. Start this 2024 with energy, enthusiasm, and excitement.

It marks a year of powerful relationship between your personality and your professional life, with such interaction being of utmost importance.

You wish to attain a position of some notoriety, and to be admired for your personal work. Success comes to a greater or lesser extent during this year, although you may consider it insufficient due to your strong ambition.

In the circle in which you operate, your presence will be evident, although others will demand responsibility from you.

In general, this period promises professional success, and you will always find the credit and protections necessary to achieve it.

Your business or professional affairs will be highlighted. Relationships with people in positions of authority, as well as with your parents, are also likely to play an important role, although a serious problem may arise that you will have to resolve.

You should develop a certain prudence in possible conflicts in the professional or business sphere.

However, it is a good time to focus on your goals and improve the image you project to the outside world.

It is a year in which you will constantly seek new experiences, but your eagerness for action and change is likely to hide a fear of establishing lasting bonds.

You will find it difficult to recognize the feminine side of your nature and accept responsibility for someone else's well-being. This year you will shy away from commitments because you don't want to feel emotionally tied down.

Others will admire your entrepreneurial spirit and appreciate that you don't skimp on responsibility, especially when one of your risky actions doesn't work out.

It is a year in which you will become a fighter who does not give up easily, and, if necessary, you will go your own way alone.

Your emotional side will be more sensitive than usual, and you will be overflowing with tenderness towards all those around you. Especially your children (if you have them) will benefit from your special predisposition to listen to them and to be more receptive to their needs, as well as more loving and understanding.

Because you appreciate the beautiful side of life more than ever, you could use this disposition for creative expression, social events, and business activities. And you are likely to initiate some sentimental relationship or change your current one in form and feeling.

You can travel more frequently to your usual places of entertainment.

Also, a family member may be able to provide you with income or financial assistance.

As far as your health is concerned, it will be a time when you will be very exposed to colds and irritations; it would not hurt to keep an eye on your respiratory tract and kidneys.

During Mercury retrograde periods consider the things, or people, you want to give a second chance to rather than starting something new. If it is something new, you may have to do it in an unconventional way.

You will meet people who are spiritually inclined and who will shape your personality. This is a good time for your spiritual awakening.

If you do not have a partner, remember that opportunities do not repeat themselves. If you are interested in a person, you should approach them and tell them how you feel without thinking twice. That small act of courage will make all the difference, the beginning of a love story.

Love

This can be a strong theme in 2024. Anything good you desire in love may be possible after May.

A planetary detox has been happening in your love life, and in your life in general. This has not been a pleasant experience. All the love experiences you have been having are of a detoxifying nature.

This year you will take a step forward in your love life and give new strength to your relationship. As a result, your relationship will be stronger than before, and the mutual trust between the two of you will increase.

During this year you will understand your partner's feelings and give importance to his or her points of view. Do not try to impose your thoughts otherwise tension may arise in your love life.

You may have to deal with unnecessary gossip, so you should be very discreet with your private life.

There will be times when you would like to break up with your partner. All of this you can control, or avoid, if you are careful about the important things in your love life.

Singles will have many opportunities to begin romantic relationships during the first three months of the year. During the second quarter, there will be fleeting relationships.

You are gradually coming to the end of a slow transformation. You must continue to take slow but steady steps forward. You must act more seriously in your relationships, and that doesn't mean you have to put aside fun.

You must be more committed to your relationship since you are practically leading a single life, but you enjoy the benefits of the existence of two. You need to learn to make decisions with your partner.

You may feel a little insecure starting in March, but it's nothing that a family getaway can't fix.

During full Moon periods you will take love more seriously and strive to become closer to those with whom you have a strong connection.

You will live some months with some uncertainty. You will start a relationship that at first will be based only on sex, however, you will become emotionally involved and confess that you are falling in love.

During this year your personal relationships become the focus of your attention. You need contact with people, and you will be concerned about their impression of you. It is time to examine your behavior in relation to other people, especially your partner, and contemplate possible adjustments and rectifications.

You may realize more than ever that you need the cooperation of others to realize your goals and that the best way to find meaning in your life, individuality and power lies in partnerships and relationships.

Participating in joint activities raises issues that will allow you to define more clearly who you are.

Your identity will be shaped and consolidated by the ups and downs and complications you encounter in trying to establish vital and sincere alliances.

Economy

This year brings a lot of positive energy for the negotiations you have been working on, especially in situations where you need to discuss important issues.

There is a chance that you may have a new position that will allow you to showcase your talents. If you have a social media presence, be sure to keep it updated.

Don't waste time and plan. If you run your own business, it's time to get out of the routine.

If you have been out of work and looking for a job, your luck improves, especially if you have specific experience or skills.

You could earn a lot of money in independent businesses that could benefit you in the future. If you are self-employed, you will also see spectacular results. You will experience some difficult moments financially during the year, but they will be mild. Those who wish to exploit their talents much more will have the possibility to do so. If you don't need to make heavy expenses, don't make them, and it won't be good for you to borrow money either. You need to start saving a lot more, as this is a complicated year.

The art of making money consists, above all, in taking advantage of opportunities. You must put the brakes on all those senseless and unordered desires and plan a better strategy to earn money. If you do not define your goals, you will not be able to succeed.

You learned many lessons regarding finances during 2023. This new year, because of all that knowledge, when you must decide, you will leave impulsiveness aside and resort to patience and tolerance. All your business dealings will bring you profits.

You will receive proposals that will allow you to choose between different beneficial options to grow in your professional area. You should carefully analyze all the details so that your final decision is the one that will bring you the most benefits.

Do not allow your mistakes to accumulate without realizing it due to your excessive passivity, if this happens the situation can become critical. This is the year to wake up and act. All the decisions you need to make are within your capabilities.

You can change your future, given free rein to your imagination. You should begin to devise projects that can generate extra income, and a new way of working.

Mercury retrograde periods will impact your professional area. This can mean that, if you don't like what you do, you will make a professional change. The time when you will feel this energy the strongest is when the solar eclipse on April 8 occurs in your career sphere.

Cancer Health

Remember that the most common health problem when the year begins is called stress. Having to deal with all the debt we have due to year-end expenses can be overwhelming. That's why it's important to be realistic and patient.

It is the perfect time for you to try things like meditation, and improve the quality of your sleep, as all of this will have many benefits for your mental health.

Remember to think positive and be optimistic as positive emotions improve energy flow.

You may suffer from allergies during this year. Do not stop making healthy changes in your diet. You should supplement your nutrition with supplements or vitamins that strengthen your immunity.

In general, your health problems may be related to nerves, excessive worrying and insufficient rest.

You may feel the need to purify your habits and become more regulated and serious. Take advantage of this year to do something for your health through sports, healthy eating, and yoga exercises.

Family

This is an important area for you. In general, it shows a move to a bigger and more spacious place, or renovation of the one you have.

Pregnancy would not be a surprise, especially if you have been trying.

Your natural compassion will manifest itself through actions directed toward those in your family circle who have lost their way and need help.

From a more understanding place, you will try to fulfill your family role, but you will do it without judging, with a more open mind, and this will make your family members take refuge in you and seek your opinion to solve family issues.

Your vital energy and will in the middle of the year seem to conflict with your emotional side, and you may have the impression that circumstances are against you, as you perceive a lack of support and affection in those around you. There may even be some tense exchanges with a beloved family member. But don't worry, this will pass quickly without substantial consequences. Being patient and flexible will help you.

Important Dates

- ***06/17 Venus enters Cancer.*** *During this transit your desire for emotional security and stability increases. You may express love and affection through acts of kindness, seeking comfort in safe environments. This is a time to strengthen bonds in existing relationships and explore shared emotional experiences.*

- ***06/17 Mercury enters Cancer.*** *This transit indicates unexpected changes at work. You will be asked to make practical moves for your personal progress, balance your income and maintain fluidity in your personal relationships.*

  Your professional area will fluctuate with negative effects, as you will not be able to utilize opportunities to their fullest potential due to a sudden change in job location.

- ***06/20 Sun enters Cancer.***

- ***07/5 New Moon in Cancer.*** *New Moons are traditionally times for new beginnings. What you start can be the focus for the next 6 months of your life.*

- ***09/ 4 to 11/3 Mars transits into Cancer**. The planet Mars in your sign generally brings a lot of energy and momentum for new beginnings and projects. This can help you jump into a new project that you will be embarking on for the next 2 years of your life.*

Monthly Horoscopes for Cancer 2024

January 2024

You start the year on the right foot, and you will not hesitate to convince your friends to accept your business proposals, even though some will find them unusual, but at the same time seductive. Your charm will take care of the rest.

January is a favorable month for initiatives focused on making changes in your family and private life. Opportunities will arise for you to evolve.

You will be inviting the person you like for a walk, if you are single, confessing that you are looking for an open relationship.

Before thinking about making more money, look for space and a change in the way you do things.

If you don't feel like sticking to your usual exercise routine, don't worry. The end of the month might be the perfect time to start another healthy habit.

There is a risk that you may be unable to tolerate situations in which all ears do not pay as much attention to you as you would like. Another problem may be the tendency to flirt with the opposite sex and have fun with unserious love games, jeopardizing an existing stable relationship.

The end of the month is a good time for important interviews, as your mental strength and creative energy operate in harmony and facilitate communication.

Also, at work you will be more effective because you have no problems to focus your forces of concentration.

You will probably feel more eager to talk than usual, and you will find it easier to get your point across than at other times.

Lucky numbers
3 - 7 - 14 - 27 - 31

February 2024

You possess a psychic ability that only needs to be strengthened a little to become a gigantic power, sometimes you can even read other people's thoughts. This ability sometimes causes you problems, but in general it works in your favor.

This month the Universe tends to change things, act fast so you can take advantage of the opportunities it provides.

Try to be careful with the way you express yourself, it is charming, but sometimes it is also aggressive.

Although you are a sign that does not hesitate to pour all your energy and enthusiasm into the pursuit of your professional goals, you must be careful not to overestimate your external achievements.

There is no doubt that professional success is important, but it would be a mistake to give your work all the attention and relegate your family obligations to the bottom of your priority list.

This month is also perfect for exploring treatments that relax your body and improve your mood. A massage with essential oils can be a heavenly experience and, if you feel exhausted, it will do you good.

As far as your health is concerned, you should especially watch your eyes, take a little more care of your skin, and control your psychic tension.

In general, you will find it difficult to reach an emotional equilibrium during this month, because you tend to have extreme and compulsive reactions. You must learn to buffer your emotional compulsion through objectivity based on reasoning.

You should especially be careful not to become emotionally involved with people who try to win your approval with their charming ways.

They have probably noticed your vulnerable nature and do not hesitate to take advantage of that weakness. Appearances can be deceiving, and it is advisable to get objective opinions about any person who awakens in you the desire to initiate an intimate sentimental relationship.

Lucky numbers
3 - 10 - 19 - 20 - 28

March 2024

Don't get too attached to dreams that may be attractive, but perhaps impossible to achieve for now. You would be wasting your energies.

Your partner may not want to share your youthful mood. There's something bothering her, you shouldn't ignore it. Plan to have a conversation. Sometimes your partner gets bored with your impertinent questions. You should try to think if the mistake is not coming from her side. The cause may be the uncertainty she feels in the relationship. Try to make a change.

You will not be in a good mood some days this month, you may feel underappreciated and that causes you anxiety. You need support, but the most important thing is that you learn to take care of yourself. You are a strong sign, and, in the end, you will be able to see what is really going on.

Singles need freedom in their relationships with other people for their personal development, therefore, they would not tolerate maintaining a bond that limits them too much. You will be constantly searching for the stimulating and fascinating, and this search influences the importance of your friends for you.

You reject normal friendship, because you desire friendly communication that allows you to forget the limitations of your daily life. With your friends you are very tolerant and open, and you are not usually possessive.

Your ideal is to live in such a way that your needs are met while having a beneficial effect on the world.

Your personal values are based on a social perspective, and you care about and are interested in the world.

You tend to be sympathetic and affectionate with most people, although your feelings often take on a diffuse form of love.

Lucky numbers
1 - 5 - 23 - 28 - 30

April 2024

There are several problems that will affect your money sector this month. You may acquire new debts, or you may borrow money from other people to finish a business deal. Try to emphasize your diet and eliminate unhealthy foods. This is a good time to start preparing your meals at home instead of eating at a restaurant every day. If you like to exercise and socialize, you should practice a sport that allows you to do both. Don't neglect your relationships. You have wonderful people who can give you good investment advice.

During this month you will feel an irresistible attraction to all that is hidden, hidden and mysterious in life. Especially the feelings and emotions that circulate through the invisible undercurrents between you and your partner will mobilize your attention.

Intimate relationships can act as catalysts that will provoke a crisis leading to transformation and renewal. In a more mundane sense, you may have some unexpected windfall during this month.

An important event will give you the courage to make some decisions that involve your quality of life and that of your family, you need to think well what to do.

Lucky numbers
1 - 10 - 12 - 18 – 21

May 2024

Throughout this month you are likely to develop your sense of responsibility and your ability to focus your full attention on a project without getting distracted.

Your main qualities in this period are precision, order, and dexterity.

You criticize and exaggerate yourself to the point of perfectionism. This month your mind will work in a cold and calculating way.

You will begin to discover new things in love, and you will be surprised by what you and your partner can do with respect to this subject, do not stop looking for ways to enrich your intimacy.

A person you don't know will give you valuable advice, don't let distrust cloud your judgment.

At work you should avoid talking about yourself or private matters, remember that this makes you respectable in front of your colleagues.

Your nature can become twofold during the month: on the one hand, you show idealistic tendencies, and you are attracted to the good for what is just and high, and on the other hand, you feel the need for movement, adventures, free life, and travel.

You can more easily establish friendships with people seduced by your enthusiasm and your communicative good humor. Your greater desire to change your environment and atmosphere makes you appreciate any change, even unfavorable, that occurs in your existence.

You prefer a more hectic and less comfortable life than a brighter destiny in immobility and stagnation.

You will feel more cheerful, even if you must face obstacles and disappointments again and again.

You may experience new financial responsibilities or could earn more money. A need to travel, to find adventure, to gain some independence and mental expansion may appear. In fact, it is an excellent time to continue your studies or to set long-term goals.

Lucky numbers
16 - 17 - 25 - 26 – 35

June 2024

This month discrepancies may appear in the group of friends with whom you normally share. This may be the result of gossip from someone outside the group.

In the middle of the month, you will feel interest in political issues, and you will show your rebellious side if someone disagrees with your opinions.

You must be careful not to delegate to your partner all the responsibility for the maintenance of the house. You must be able to empathize with her.

It is a period where you should take an inventory of your potential talents and analyze if there are any that you have left aside and that are worth exploiting.

You intend to celebrate a big event this month, but it is likely that you will have to postpone the celebration. This is not the time to spend on celebrations, it is better to wait for the right moment.

The end of the month can be seen as cursed, as you will probably receive bad news at work. You should not get discouraged, try to think positively.

If you have doubts about a situation that has the potential to affect you, you should inquire to see what is going on. Do not be afraid, think that many times people do not want to tell the whole truth, but there are things you need to know and for that you should ask.

Someone at work does something wrong and you feel like telling your superiors about it. That is not a healthy idea, the best thing to do is to talk directly to the person.

You should never go to sleep anxious or upset because that way stress and anxiety intoxicate your sleep and you do not rest.

Lucky numbers
11 - 17 - 18 - 23 - 24

July 2024

This month you will feel a little insecure at work, and disappointments await you in your professional life. Because of your indiscipline and irresponsibility, you may have a bad time.

You should not consume any drug; these bad habits only cloud your vision. Do not assume escapist attitudes.

During this period, you will feel an inner emptiness in your life, you will have the feeling that something is missing. The solution is to look for answers in your subconscious and discover aspects that are dormant.

In the middle of the month, you will be caught in a conflict between your personal and professional life, and you will have to sacrifice part of your work time to solve urgent personal problems.

You will behave in an intellectual manner and will want to substantiate your ideas and opinions. You will take on more educational activities or pursue research that may serve this purpose.

It is a time when you will become familiar with a variety of techniques and points of view that will enable you to compare and judge theories, concepts, and methods based on your own personal experience.

You may wonder what aspects of yourself you should change if you don't have a partner and what you should do to make that person you are interested in approach you in a romantic tone. The answer is to use your sympathy and be yourself. Don't wear masks.

Lucky numbers
1 - 6 - 12 - 15 – 20

August 2024

If you want to avoid conflicts this month you must learn to play by the rules. Avoid watching that person you are interested in their social networks. If he/she finds out about it, he/she won't like it.

To be able to relate to others you must recognize that they also have the right to express themselves freely as you do. Otherwise, coexistence will be impossible.

During this period, you will put more effort than usual into your work. It is a time when you will be analyzing different possibilities in your profession, and possibilities of starting a business will arise.

You have the strength to rise to the top. Moderate your domineering attitude, as it can cause problems in your profession. If you get carried away by your ambition to succeed, you will commit inconsiderate actions.

You will want to get back into the rhythm of your life. Last month you had to deal with a lot of changes, but this month you want your life to be balanced again. This month is likely to be stable if you learn to pace yourself.

Try to give up routine daily activities and replace them with exciting things to spice up your relationship.

It is also important to strengthen ties with your friends and family. Don't be too impulsive, be subtle, help more without being aggressive. Details make the difference in many relationships.

In your workplace, certain colleagues may try to annoy you. It is imperative that you ignore them completely, these are absurd whims.

Your work is the only thing you need to pay attention to, so be sure to work focused so that you can achieve success. When facing anyone, keep a positive approach.

Lucky numbers
1 - 12 - 19 - 24 - 28

September 2024

This month your emotional world will be turbulent, and extremely unstable as far as your love life is concerned. You must remember that variety is not a guarantee of satisfaction. Constant change in your personal relationships can result in frustration and nervous disorders.

You will have the ability to keep your finances in order. Your bank accounts will look quite healthy. You have saved and will have extra money for fun.

It will be important to exercise, but also pay attention to your hobbies, as this will keep your mind strong and active.

Health will be quite good because you will feel energetic. Due to the intensity of this month, your health may suffer a little. Recreational activities will help you maintain a good physical and mental balance.

Your circle of friends will expand, but you will feel a superficial commitment to them.

It is important for you to learn that a favorable personal relationship is a two-way thing. You cannot expect the other person to do everything you want, while you maintain your absolute freedom. Moreover, if you apply such a negative attitude to your profession, the result will be catastrophic.

You possess a shrewd mentality and, at times, can become so astute that you are prone to deception. Your extreme sensitivity gives you the ability to guess what others are trying to do.

This month self-deception may arise in you because your imagination will move away from the world in which we live, which may lead you to confuse your fantasies with reality.

At times, you feel discouraged and lack self-confidence because you are overly sensitive and worry for no reason. Your personal relationships may deteriorate because of your propensity to live in unreality.

Some unforeseen expenses may appear, these will not only be unavoidable, but will put your bank account close to zero.

Try to control your expenses, if you don't want to have financial problems during this month you should not ask for any loan.

You need to plan your finances and establish a budget. Avoid any legal problems.

Lucky numbers
9 - 17 - 22 - 25 - 28

October 2024

This month changes will make you feel overwhelmed, and you will want to change your life drastically. It is advisable that you make new approaches in your life.

You will try to make drastic decisions for your career and lifestyle. Be sure to use your energy correctly so that you can get the best and be successful. Your emotions can push you down the wrong path, so make sure they are in check.

Possible concerns about past problems. Loss or death near you.

You may have to pay fines.

The relationship you are in could end out of spite. You can avoid that if you make the right decisions. Maintain transparency in your love life by maintaining a good level of communication to avoid misunderstandings. It will be imperative that you listen to your partner if you want the relationship to last.

It will also be a favorable month for those who are planning to have a child.

If you are single, you may find potential partners.

The workload at the end of the month will be heavy. You should not get tense; all you need to do is work hard and you will keep everything under control.

At the end of the month, you will find yourself in a difficult situation in which you will have to spend money on your closest relatives. It will be a tense situation, for that reason you must remain calm.

Lucky numbers
2 - 6 - 34 - 35 - 36

November 2024

This month money will become your source of stress, you are ending the period of good financial health and beginning a low period. It will be a period of constant changes in your personal economy, and you will have to get rid of material things to be able to face your outstanding debts.

As if that were not enough, this month you may also experience events such as the death of a family member or close friend.

Your way of being, and your behavior will undergo a metamorphosis. Your life begins a new and different chapter because all extreme events will lead you to make extreme modifications. You may even change your residence.

Try to be perseverant with your resolutions because all these influences will lead you to change your mentality several times.

You must maintain balance and not become materialistic, leaving other values in your life aside.

Expect many twists and turns in your profession. But you will still be presented with a variety of opportunities that you can use to get out of any backlog.

Make sure you take advantage of every professional opportunity and that your personal activities are not diversified.

You must take care of your mental health. Make sure you don't stress yourself out, as this could be the reason you suffer a nervous breakdown.

Watch your stress levels and try to be mentally strong. Exercise without pushing your limits.

Lucky numbers
3 - 4 - 12 - 18 - 28

December 2024

If you have a partner, you will realize that your relationship needs some changes in the daily routine. Failure to do so will result in disagreements due to the limitations of a very measured life. If your lifestyle is too orderly, then there will be a danger of a breakup or separation.

If you don't have a partner, you will meet unusual people unexpectedly. There is a tendency this month to have passing or extravagant romances.

Legal matters will have unexpected changes and the outcome will be surprising. If you are involved in politics or anything related to economics, you will face defamations.

This month marks the end of one professional stage and the beginning of a different one. If you are an adult, it could be the year of your retirement. If you are young, the possibilities are different, it could be the culmination of your career.

At the end of the month all the business you start will be fruitful, but you will see the results next year.

Your new goals will be influenced by your family, they will be aimed at consolidating your position and greater stability.

Be careful with forbidden loves or secret relationships that will complicate your well-being, especially if you already have a formal partner.

You should try to raise your self-esteem and analyze the conditions of your present affective life so that you can cancel the inferiority complexes.

As the end of the year approaches, there may be some confusion about your career decisions, so stay true to yourself and continue to work consistently.

The planets will move into favorable positions in 2025, and it will be a good year from a professional point of view. The ambitions you have will come to success if you continue to move in the right direction.

If you have financial commitments, make sure you keep them so you can stay away from risks. You must try and save money.

The coming year 2025 predicts a lower stress load. Plan your finances and keep control over your expenses.

Lucky numbers
2 - 7 - 23 - 27 - 32

The Tarot Cards, an Enigmatic and Psychological World.

The word Tarot means "royal road", it is a millenary practice, it is not known exactly who invented card games in general, nor the Tarot in particular; there are the most dissimilar hypotheses in this sense.

Some say that it arose in Atlantis or Egypt, but others believe that tarots came from China or India, from the ancient land of the gypsies, or that they arrived in Europe through the Cathars. The fact is that tarot cards distill astrological, alchemical, esoteric, and religious symbolism, both Christian and pagan.

Until recently, if you mentioned the word 'tarot' to some people, it was common for them to imagine a gypsy sitting in front of a crystal ball in a room surrounded by mysticism, or to think of black magic or witchcraft, but nowadays this has changed.

This ancient technique has been adapting to the new times, it has joined technology and many young people feel a deep interest in it.

Young people have isolated themselves from religion because they believe that they will not find the solution to what they need there, they realized the duality of this, something that does not happen with spirituality. All over the social networks you find accounts dedicated to the study and tarot readings, since everything related to esotericism is fashionable, in fact, some hierarchical decisions are made considering the tarot or astrology.

What is remarkable is that the predictions that are usually related to tarot are not the most sought after, the ones related to self-knowledge and spiritual counseling are the most requested.

The tarot is an oracle, through its drawings and colors, we stimulate our psychic sphere, the innermost part that goes beyond the natural. Many people turn to the tarot as a spiritual or psychological guide because we live in uncertain times, and this pushes us to seek answers in spirituality.

It is such a powerful tool that tells you concretely what is going on in your subconscious so that you can perceive it through the lens of a new wisdom.

Carl Gustav Jung, the famed psychologist, used the symbols of tarot cards in his psychological studies.

He created the theory of archetypes, where he discovered an extensive sum of images that help in analytical psychology.

The use of drawings and symbols to appeal to a deeper understanding is frequently used in psychoanalysis. These allegories are part of us, corresponding to symbols of our subconscious and our mind.

Our unconscious has dark areas, and when we use visual techniques, we can reach different parts of it and reveal elements of our personality that we do not know. When you can decode these messages through the pictorial language of tarot, you can choose what decisions to make in life to create the destiny you really want.

The tarot with its symbols teaches us that a different universe exists, especially nowadays where everything is so chaotic, and a logical explanation is sought for everything.

The Moon, Tarot Card for Cancer 2024

You can be deceived, lie to yourself or act fraudulently towards others.

This card represents separation, sudden changes, and disappointment.

Be careful, many things you may not know may be happening around you.

Use your telepathy and intuition. It indicates that you may be in a period where your emotions come to the surface more easily.

This card indicates dreams, the occult, the feminine part of every human being that is present at this stage.

The best thing you can do is to express your emotions as naturally and evenly as possible.

Don't be afraid of pain and enjoy joy with intensity. This card also represents secret enemies, so listen to your intuition, especially in business and love.

It can mean reconciliations with friends or family members from whom you have been somewhat estranged, if perhaps there was a breakup.

It may also symbolize that your inner emotional turmoil is being resolved.

Runes of the Year 2024

Runes are a set of symbols that form an alphabet. "Rune" means secret and symbolizes the sound of one stone colliding with another. Runes are a visionary and magical method.

Runes are not used for exact predictions, but they are used to guide you about a future event, issue, or decision. Runes have specific symbolism for the person who wants it, and messages related to challenges in life.

MANNAZ, Rune of Cancer 2024

This rune tells you that to understand others, you must first understand yourself. It predicts that there are changes on your path. It reminds you that, although you want to change others, you cannot, only you can transform yourself. Be true to your principles and to those around you. In this way, you will get to know yourself and you will be able to explore reality more accurately. Focus on the here and now.

This year 2024 demands your inner advancement. Try to change so that you can adapt to this new environment. This rune reminds you that the origin of transformation is yourself, so be ready to accept the changes of heart.

You are living in a somewhat nebulous period, so you must remember that the soil is fertilized first before cultivating it, in short, you must be patient.

Look into your subconscious, discover your weaknesses, appreciate your attributes and control how you communicate. You must be sincere and judge yourself with dignity. This rune is linked to simplicity, advising you to concentrate on your duties with respect.

Mannaz announces the arrival of a period of personal growth in which the starting point will be a new approach and a new way of acting and looking at problems.

Lucky Colors

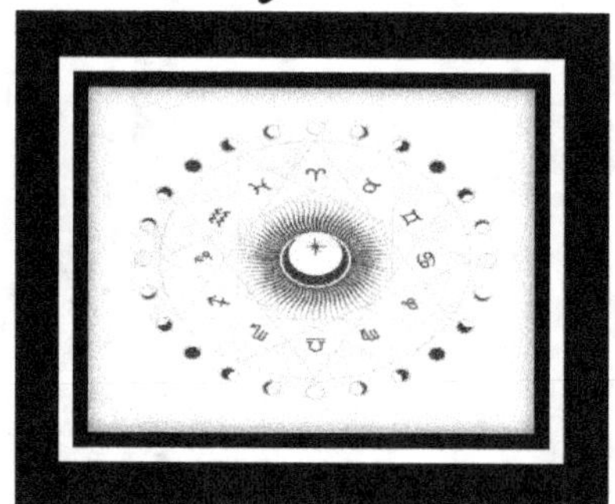

Colors affect us psychologically; they influence our appreciation of things, opinion about something or someone, and can be used to influence our decisions.

Traditions to welcome the new year vary from country to country, and on the night of December 31 we take stock of all the positive and negative things we experienced in the year that is leaving. We start thinking about what to do to transform our luck in the new year ahead.

There are several ways to attract positive energies towards us when we receive the new year, and one of them is to wear or wear accessories of a specific color that attracts what we wish for the year to begin.

Colors have energetic charges that influence our lives, so it is always advisable to receive the year dressed in a color that attracts the energies of what we want to achieve.

For that there are colors that vibrate positively with each zodiac sign, so the recommendation is that you wear the clothes with the hue that will make you attract prosperity, health, and love in 2024. (These colors can also be used during the rest of the year for important occasions, or to enhance your days).

Remember that, although the most common is to wear red underwear for passion, pink for love and yellow or gold for abundance, it is never too much to include in our attire the color that most benefits our zodiac sign.

Cancer

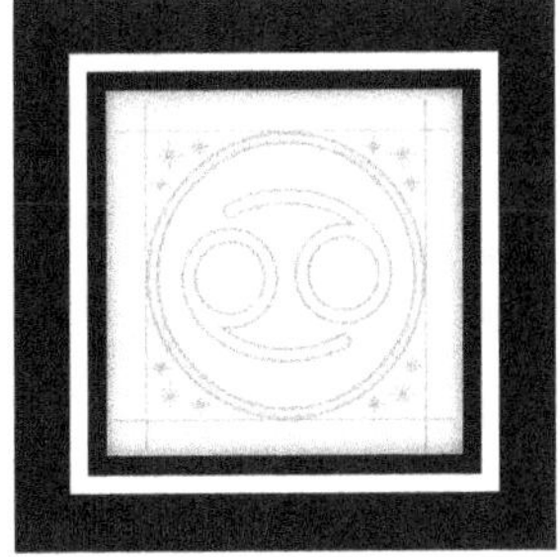

Red

The key words for red are Attraction, love, passion, desire, love.

Red symbolizes power. This color is related to vitality and ambition. It is also related to strength, determination, and power, and is used to attract attention.

Red brings confidence, courage, and an optimistic attitude towards life.

It has a negative aspect: it can express anger. If we are surrounded by too much red, it can influence us negatively and make us irritable, impatient, and non-conformist.

If you wear red you will feel confident and ready to attract attention wherever you enter. Even if you lack self-confidence, your aura will absorb the positive energy of red, and everyone will be attracted to you.

There is a phenomenon called the "red effect" which suggests that people who use color influence the perceptions of others.

Lucky charms

Who doesn't own a lucky ring, a chain that never comes off, or an object that they wouldn't give away for anything in the world? We all attribute a special power to certain items that belong to us and that special character that they assume for us makes them magical objects.

For a talisman to act and influence circumstances, its bearer must have faith in it, and this will transform it into a prodigious object, able to accomplish everything that is asked of it.

In the everyday sense an amulet is any object that propitiates good as a preventive measure against evil, harm, disease, and witchcraft.

Good luck charms can help you to have a year 2024 full of blessings in your home, work, with your family, attract money and health.

For the amulets to work properly you should not lend them to anyone else, and you should always have them at hand.

Amulets have existed in all cultures and are made from elements of nature that serve as catalysts of energies that help create human desires.

The amulet is assigned the power to ward off evils, spells, diseases, disasters or to counteract evil wishes cast through the eyes of others.

Cancer Amulet

The Ankh Egyptian Cross

The Egyptian cross, one of the oldest and most important amulets of Ancient Egypt, signifies life and immortality.

A talisman that will give you strength, abundance, and protection against bad luck. It is believed that the Egyptians used it as an amulet for good health. This was an amulet used during life and carried to the grave.

It has magical properties and is also known as "the Egyptian key of wisdom". It has the power to help people understand all the secrets of the universe.

This protective amulet is a repellent of evil and negative energies.

Lucky Quartz

We are all attracted to diamonds, rubies, emeralds and sapphires, obviously precious stones. Semi-precious stones such as carnelian, tiger's eye, white quartz, and lapis lazuli are also highly prized as they have been used as ornaments and symbols of power for thousands of years.

What many do not know is that they were valued for more than their beauty: each had a sacred significance, and their healing properties were as important as their ornamental value.

Crystals still have the same properties in our days, most people are familiar with the most popular ones such as amethyst, malachite and obsidian, but nowadays there are new crystals such as larimar, petalite and phenacite that have become known.

A crystal is a solid body with a geometrically regular shape, crystals were formed when the earth was created and have continued to metamorphose as the planet has changed, crystals are the DNA of the earth, they are miniature stores that contain the development of our planet over millions of years.

Some have been bent to extraordinary pressures and others grew in chambers buried deep underground, others dripped into being. Whatever form they take, their crystalline structure can absorb, conserve, focus and emit energy.

At the heart of the crystal is the atom, its electrons, and protons. The atom is dynamic and is composed of a series of particles that rotate around the center in constant motion, so that, although the crystal may seem motionless, it is a living molecular mass that vibrates at a certain frequency, and this is what gives energy to the crystal.

Gems used to be a royal and priestly prerogative, the priests of Judaism wore a plaque on their chest full of precious stones which was much more than an emblem to designate their function, as it transferred power to the wearer.

Men have worn stones since the stone age as they had a protective function guarding their wearers from various evils. Today's crystals have the same power, and we can select our jewelry not only according to their external attractiveness, having them near us can boost our energy (orange carnelian), clean the space around us (amber) or attract wealth (citrine).

Certain crystals such as smoky quartz and black tourmaline could absorb negativity, emitting a pure and clean energy.

Wearing a black tourmaline around the neck protects from electromagnetic emanations including that of cell phones, a citrine will not only attract wealth, but will also help you keep it, place it in the wealthy part of your home (the back left most away from the front door).

If you are looking for love, crystals can help you, place a rose quartz in the relationship corner of your house (the back right corner furthest away from the front door) its effect is so powerful that you may want to add an amethyst to offset the attraction.

You can also use rhodochrosite, love will come your way.

Crystals can heal and give balance, some crystals contain minerals known for their therapeutic properties, malachite has a high concentration of copper, wearing a malachite bracelet allows the body to absorb minimal amounts of copper.

Lapis lazuli relieves migraine, but if the headache is caused by stress, amethyst, amber or turquoise placed above the eyebrows will relieve it.

Quartz and minerals are jewels of mother earth, give yourself the opportunity, and connect with the magic they give off.

Lucky Quartz for Cancer 2024

Onyx

A protective quartz that cleanses the aura. According to legend, this stone emerged when Venus was sleeping and Cupid cut her nails, so that they fell to the ground and these nails were transmuted into wonderful stones that were baptized Onyx.

In times of stress, it helps to make prudent decisions, and to achieve your professional goals if you use it as an amulet.

It is a powerful stone, with psychological benefits that make it an admirable choice to provide support for people suffering from anxiety. Its properties will connect you with your spiritual guides, and you will be able to see everything more clearly.

Compatibility of Cancer and the Zodiac Signs

Cancer is a water sign symbolized by a crab that walks between the sea and its shore, a capacity that is also reflected in its ability to merge emotional and physical states.

Cancer's intuition that comes from its emotional side manifests itself in a tangible way, and as security and honesty are paramount for this sign, it can be a bit cold and distant at first.

Cancer reveals her gentle spirit little by little, and her genuine compassion and psychic abilities. If you are fortunate and earn their trust, you will discover that, despite their initial shyness, they love to share.

For this lover, a partner is truly the greatest gift and he rewards relationships with his indestructible loyalty, responsibility, and emotional support. He tends to be quite homely, and his home is a personal temple, an area in which he can express his personality.

With its domestic capabilities, the crab is also a sublime host. Don't be surprised if your Cancer partner likes to flatter you with home-cooked meals because there's nothing, he loves more than natural food. Cancer is also very anxious about his friends and family; he loves to take on guardian roles that allow him to create passionate bonds with his closest companions. But never forget that when Cancer invests in someone emotionally, they run the risk of blurring the line between caring and control.

Cancer also has a fickle nature like the Moon and a propensity for instability. Cancer is the sullenest sign of the zodiac. Their partners must learn to appreciate their emotional variations, and of course Cancer must also control their own sentimentality.

His defensive habits have a flip side and when he feels provoked, he will not hesitate to get defensive. Cancer should remember that occasional mistakes and quarrels do not make your partner your enemy. In addition, you should strive energetically to be present in your relationships.

As an emotional and introspective sign, it is easy for them to withdraw into themselves most of the time and if they don't stay present in a relationship, the next time they come out of their shell, their partner may no longer be by their side. Cancer is a good listener, and once he comes out of his shell, he is an emotional sponge. Your Cancer partner will absorb your emotions, which can sometimes be supportive, but other times can be suffocating. It's not easy to tell if Cancer is mimicking or really empathizing with you, but since they are so interconnected with their partner, it makes no difference.

If Cancer's emotional backing is getting in the way of your personality, it's best to let it go. This sensitive sign is easily challenged by even the subtlest opinion, and although he avoids direct conflict by walking at angles, he can also use his molars.

This characteristically carefree and provocative behavior is to be expected, and it is rare to date Cancer without getting a taste of his characteristically bad temper at least once.

Because of Cancer's sensitivity, it is not easy to argue with him, but over time you will learn what words to say, and perhaps more importantly, what to avoid. Be aware of what bothers your partner, and over time, it will become easier to have difficult dialogues. It is important to know how this magical creature works at its best and worst times. Ultimately, the most important thing to remember is that Cancer is never as indifferent as it looks.

The most difficult thing with Cancer is to break through its hard and rigid surface. For this reason, tolerance is key when flirting with Cancer. Keep a slow and steady pace, and over time you will gain the confidence to reveal your true self. Of course, this can be a long and complicated process, and the slightest mistake can put Cancer on the defensive, so two steps forward can turn into one step back. Don't be discouraged, it's not personal, it's just the physiology of a crab.

Cancer can have casual sex, but this sweet water sign prefers relationships that have emotional intimacy.

Remember that Cancer needs to be completely comfortable before coming out of its shell, and this is especially important when it comes to sexuality. For the crab, trust is fueled by physical proximity. You can begin to cultivate a sexual relationship with Cancer by slowly integrating little by little, allowing for their pace, and caresses. This will allow Cancer to become more comfortable with merging emotional and physical expression, making sure he feels protected before you start making love.

Although Cancer is patient and tends to be extremely loyal, as they need to feel protected, and understood by their partner, they may seek intimacy with another person if they feel these demands are not met.

Cancer can be very mischievous, so any secret relationship will be calculated, and a stray crab will make it necessary to take his mischief to the grave, he will take extra measures to prevent the encounter from being discovered by burying the evidence on the seashore.

In fact, even the most loyal crab will have secrets, but that doesn't mean they're bad or evil. Everyone deserves to keep certain things private, plus a little mystery will add a touch to the relationship.

Cancer does not find it easy to establish a serious and committed relationship, and when he feels secure, he will not want it to break up.

Cancer tends to stay in relationships even after the sparks have perished because quite simply, Cancer is sentimental at heart. But, of course, not all relationships are meant to last forever.

This water sign does not pretend to be vindictive, but when his heart is broken, he knows how to set boundaries. Deleting your phone number, blocking you and unfollowing you on social media allow him to protect himself from pain during a breakup. So, if your relationship with Cancer comes to an end, expect to receive a thorough list of rules. Cancer can be idealistic, and this water sign is undoubtedly looking for his transcript of a romance. However, it interacts dissimilarly with each zodiac sign.

Cancer and Aries are a *difficult relationship. The ambitious attitude of Aries differs with the deep tenderness of Cancer. As a result, Aries may feel stifled by Cancer's neediness, and Cancer may feel abandoned by Aries' positivistic nature.*

Cancer also resents direct conflict and, like its astrological symbol, the crab, prefers to dodge difficult situations rather than face conflict head-on, which is the more common Aries way. Aries is not very friendly to these passive tendencies, so this relationship can sometimes prove difficult.

When paired with Aries, Cancer must embrace a more direct approach to conflict resolution. Aries will esteem your composure, and this reasoning will allow both signs to create an indestructible union. If they learn to respect, they can look forward to a long-lasting relationship, based on love, and support.

Cancer and Taurus *are both romantic and know how to give each other the emotional support they need. Although they tend to be possessive, Taurus brings security and loyalty to the sensitive Cancer, and Cancer's gentle seductive style attracts him.*

Friction only arises when the two begin to reproach each other. If Cancer is assiduously grinding its tongs, Taurus will start bottling up its resentments something that will end up erupting into a titanic bullfight. Favorably, they can avoid tensions by maintaining honest communication and appreciating each other's gifts.

Cancer and Gemini *are a fun relationship. The sensitive, watery Cancer needs a lot of affection from their partner to feel secure and loved. At first, you'll question how the spontaneous Gemini, who enjoys so much freedom to explore his or her diverse interests, can fit in. However, as a mutable air sign, he is also very flexible.*

If Cancer can give clear notice of their requirements, Gemini will work to meet them. Gemini can also be quite indifferent and reclusive, while Cancer is a sea-spout of emotions, but if Gemini is willing to empathize with Cancer, this can be an affectionate and quite entertaining relationship.

***Cancer and Cancer**, it can be a lasting relationship. When two crustaceans connect, it's quite a love affair. Sensitive and instinctive they know how to facilitate the emotional support that the other aspires.*

They are both homebodies and will enjoy spending time together, cuddling in bed, or on the couch, or creating a cozy atmosphere in the place they share. However, difficulties can arise when they get too comfortable.

If these oceanic lovers remember to encourage each other and open their hard shells to trust each other fully, this can be an immortal relationship.

***Cancer and Leo**, not exactly an easy match, doesn't mean it's unlikely, because as strange as it may seem, the crab and the lion have a lot in common. In their own way, both Cancer and Leo demand love, gratitude, and validation.*

While the dramatic Leo seeks compliments and loyalty, the sensitive Cancer wants to be needed and understood. The recipe for conflict between these signs is obvious.

Leo being so dramatic and craving the applause of his environment, coupled with Cancer, homebody, results in the latter feeling unloved which leads Leo to take Cancer's dryness personally and here they begin to quarrel.

However, if both Cancer and Leo manage their feelings, it is not difficult to avoid this type of conflict.

An open dialogue and a lot of tenderness will help to strengthen this romantic relationship.

***Cancer and Virgo**, although there are obvious differences between them, because Cancer is moved by emotions, while Virgo is moved by logic, they can make a vigorous couple, even if they must be fooled a little.*

As Cancer and Virgo get to know each other, the relationship has many stumbles and moves forward and backward frequently. However, once trust is instituted, this couple is truly deep. Although neither is attracted to talking about their feelings at first, if both are equally involved, they can find security in their mutual respect and self-confidence.

***Cancer and Libra**, at the beginning of the courtship, Cancer's withdrawn attitude confuses Libra, who works tirelessly to try to impress the surly crustacean. In contrast, Libra's communication and highly flirtatious demeanor make Cancer wary of her intentions.*

Sarcastically, both Cancer and Libra fear that the other sign will get on their nerves. However, once Cancer accepts Libra's particularity, and Libra understands Cancer's tender spirit, the two can relate harmoniously.

Cancer and Scorpio, *belonging to the water element, have a pasty relationship here. Cancer is a considerably sensitive creature, so it needs to establish familiarity and loyalty before revealing its weaknesses.*

Consequently, like-minded Scorpio is a wonderful partner for the delicate crustacean.

This connection is based on deep intuition and psychic abilities, so Cancer and Scorpio can often communicate with non-verbal forms of expression. Cancer and Scorpio can be very impulsive, both carry a lot of emotions, but they know how to help each other, lighting the way for their darker moments. In the end, they both seek the same thing: intimacy.

Scorpio is very possessive, so Cancer should be able to adapt by repeatedly showing their love.

Cancer and Scorpio love the good life. Having a majestic home and adorned with luxuries.

Cancer and Sagittarius, *a difficult but not impossible relationship at first, each of these two very different energies may be attracted to the other's differences.*

Sagittarius talks fast, and is bolstered by Cancer's spirit, while the crustacean is bewitched by the effortless delicacy of the optimistic Sagittarius. Sagittarius' need for adventure does not mesh well with Cancer's homey desires.

In a couple with people of these signs Cancer should remember that the house is not a territory, but a state of mind.

Likewise, Sagittarius will have to understand that stability does not mean dungeon. If they are willing to change their appreciations a little, there are high expectations for this relationship.

Cancer and Capricorn, *although astrologically opposite, share similar values: both cares deeply about family and friends, and about building a sustainable future. Although seemingly less emotional than Cancer, the hard-working Capricorn deeply appreciates Cancerian sensitivity.*

For its part, Cancer's intuition can bring a much-needed spirituality to Capricorn's practicality.

The Cancer-Capricorn relationship is perfect because both signs enjoy nesting and building safe spaces.

However, as both fear change, Cancer and Capricorn must work hard to keep their relationship from stagnating.

After all, they don't need to curl up by the fire every night of the week. It's also okay to have fun outside from time to time.

***Cancer and Aquarius**, although this relationship may seem strange at first (Cancer is quite traditional, while Aquarius is extremely progressive), both signs are innovative thinkers with brilliant ideas on how to live creatively and impactfully in the world.*

Their perspectives, however, are very different. Cancer's views always reflect their immediate reality, while Aquarius theorizes at 30,000 feet. As a result, there may be some discord in a Cancer-Aquarius couple.

They should strive to ensure that everyone's needs are considered.

***Cancer and Pisces**, it is a relationship where the crab can finally find its passionate partner. If there is one thing that connects a fish and a crab, it is that both give love the most important position in their lives.*

They both believe that love is the driving force that gives us the strength to function in life.

The strength of the passion they both feel for their partners makes them run and fall into each other's arms.

The only difficulty is that Pisces always walks in the clouds and ignores the future, something that is fundamental for Cancer.

If the crustacean does not see his plans come to fruition, he chooses to break off the relationship.

But in general, they have similar feelings which will make them an envied couple.

They both love to share intimately, and the warmth of Cancer and Pisces suggests a committed relationship in which it will be easy to reach a consensus.

Cancer and Vocation

As a lawyer or psychoanalyst, Cancer can help people. Oceanography is particularly one of Cancer's vocations as the crab is their zodiac symbol with a strong connection to the sea. Being a chef or baker would allow them to exercise their creative skills and nurture their customers with their meals.

Best Professions

Cancer is tough on the outside, but very gentle on the inside. This sign ruled by the Moon is very enigmatic. They are very energetic, imaginative, and protective. Cancer excels in the professions of nursing, psychology, law, education, and adult care.

Signs not to do business with

Aquarius and Gemini, because Cancer is prone to live in the past, Aquarius and Gemini never look back. They do not understand each other and recharge each other with negative vibrations.

Signs to be associated with

Pisces and Sagittarius. They are versatile signs that adapt to all circumstances. They are very good at finding clients and contacts.

Money Rituals

Ritual for Cash Flow

You need:

- 2 silver coins of any denomination

- 1 clear glass container

- Sacred Water

- Sea salt

- Fresh milk

- Amethyst stone

Add the sacred water and sea salt to the container. Place the coins in the water and repeat in your mind: "You cleanse and purify yourself; you make me prosperous". Two days later you remove the coins from the water, go to the garden, and dig a hole and bury the coins and the amethyst. If you do not have a garden, bury them somewhere where there is soil.

When you have buried the coins, before closing the hole, pour fresh milk over them. Think about the amount of money you wish to get. Once you have expressed your wishes, you can cover the hole. Try to hide it as well as possible so that no one digs there again.

After six weeks, dig up the coins and the amethyst, keep them with you always as amulets.

Spell to Alter Money Flow.

You need:

- 1 silver coin of any value

- 1 glass container

- Sacred water or Full Moon water

- Sea salt

- 1 gold or silver candle

- 1 needle

- Matches

Add the water and salt in the container. Place the coin in the water, and repeat: "You purify yourself and make me rich". Then you take the coin out of the water and dry it.

You take the candle, and with the needle, you write on it the symbol of money $$$". With the candle in your hands, you repeat: "This candle brings me money". Light the candle and drop a few drops of wax on the coin. Then you place the candle on the coin, so that it sticks.

Once the candle and the coin are glued, you repeat your economic petition saying: "By the power of fire, by the energies of this candle, by the golden or silver color I become a magnet for money. May my will be fulfilled. May it be so, it is so, and it shall be so."

Spell to Increase Abundance.

You need:

- 3 white candles

- 2 orange candles

- 4 oranges (fruits)

- 1 new sewing needle

- Matches

Start this spell on a Sunday at sunrise. You take a white candle, and with the needle you write your name on it.

Cut the orange, eat a small piece. Light your candle and repeat in your mind: "As I eat this fruit, I ingest the power of Ra" Let the candle burn out.

You repeat this ritual in the same way and at the same time on the following two Sundays.

On the last Sunday of the month the ritual has a slight difference.

You take the two orange candles, and hold them in the direction of the rising Sun while repeating:

"Mighty Ra, may these candles endure with your power."

You light the candles, and next to them you place a completely peeled orange.

Lift the orange, and repeat:

"With this I connect your power with mine."

You let the candles burn out.

Spell to Attract Abundance.

You need:

- 1 orange (fruit)

- 1 photograph of you

- Cinnamon powder

- Black tourmaline

You take the orange and cut it in half, place your photo in the middle.

Open a hole in your yard or garden and place the orange inside, sprinkle the cinnamon on top of the orange and repeat:

"As the sun shines so will I shine until the end of my life". Place the tourmaline and close the hole.

When the earth accepts your offering, and the orange disintegrates, your aura will be a magnet for money.

Business Cleansing Spell.

You need:

- Egg shell

- 1 bouquet of white flowers

- Sacred water or Full Moon water

- Milk

- Cinnamon Powder

- New cleaning bucket

- New mop

You start by sweeping your home or business from the inside to the outside of the street repeating in your mind to let the negative out and the positive in.

You mix all the ingredients in the bucket and wipe the floor from the inside to the outside of the street door.

You let the floor dry and sweep the flowers towards the street door, pick them up and throw them in the trash along with the bucket and mop. Do not touch anything with your hands. You should do this once a week, preferably at the time of the planet Jupiter.

Spell to Cleanse your Business of Bad Vibrations.

You need:

- 1 bunch of parsley

- 1 bunch of basil

- Honey

- Sea salt

- 1 glass of white rum

- 1 earthenware pot

Put both branches in a blender together with the honey, the salt, and the glass of rum. Blend them for three minutes.

You separate the liquid into three equal parts. Pour one part in front of the door of the business. The other parts should be kept inside the store in a clay container, and the rest, well covered, should be kept in the refrigerator.

The ritual must be repeated for a month, every Sunday and Thursday of the week.

Spell to Protect your Business from Theft.

You need:

- 1 copper vessel

- 90 proof alcohol

- 10 drops of eucalyptus oil

- 10 drops of lavender oil

- 1 sprig of rue

- 1 amethyst

You must macerate in the container all the ingredients immersed in the alcohol during a complete phase of Crescent Moon.

Every day, as soon as it gets dark, you will shake the mixture. After this Lunation, you will transfer the liquid from the container to the vaporizer bottle and introduce the amethyst. With this you can fumigate all the corners of the rooms in your home or office.

Ritual to Improve at Work.

You need:

- 3 green candles

- 2 white candles

- 2 yellow candles

- 1 paper cartridge

You place the candles in a circle, clockwise, first the green ones, then the white ones, then the yellow ones.

Write your requests on the paper and place it folded in the center of the circle. Light the candles and repeat seven times: "I have strength and faith; I direct my life towards abundance". This ritual should be done at least twice a week before going to work. Preferably on Tuesdays and Thursdays.

Ritual to Change Jobs.

You need:

- 1 dark green candle.

- 1 red candle.

- 1 a purple candle

- 1 piece of paper with the details of the job you want to obtain or change.

You light the candles forming a pyramid and place the folded paper in the center. Repeat seven times: "I am fine with what I have, but I wish to be better, in a place more in accordance with my tastes and expectations.

Therefore, I pray to my guardian angel to help me in this quest". Repeat this seven times. This ritual should be performed before leaving for work.

Best Countries and Cities to Live In

Countries: *The Netherlands, Canada, England, Australia, Denmark, Venezuela, Mexico, Argentina, Cuba, Portugal, and Guatemala.*

Cities: *Moscow, Havana, Berlin, Lisbon, Cartagena, Sao Paulo, Rio de Janeiro, Medellin, Madrid, and London.*

Incense and Essential Oils for Money

Plants for Money

Eucalyptus: just burn a few leaves and walk around the house, so that the aroma spreads in every room, eliminating bad energies and letting in abundance.

Quartz for Money

Lapis Lazuli: *It is a protective and powerful quartz against bad energies. In Egypt it was placed in the tombs to take care of the dead in the afterlife. It attracts professional success.*

Money Charms

The Pentacles of Jupiter that will guarantee you Prosperity.

Pentacles are magical figures, capable of transmitting positive energies to their environment. The action of Jupiter's pentacles derives from the combination of letters, signs, and beneficial formulas, they symbolize graphically and mystically a wish.

They clearly act on the psyche of people who have visual contact with him.

The largest compilation of pentacles is found in The Clavicles of King Solomon, a volume of high magic attributed to this biblical king. In it are 36 pentacles that have various purposes and among them are the seven pentacles of Jupiter.

Pentacles to Prosper.

The purpose of these pentacles is to provide abundance, to resolve work-related conflicts and to assist in receiving more directly all kinds of benefits that grant greater prosperity.

Jupiter, the so-called Great Benefic in astrology, is a planet that is related to expansion, optimism, links with powerful people and the ability to make fortune.

 You should draw them with great concentration and with the intention that they manifest your will. The most suitable material is a piece of parchment. Once finished, they should be hung somewhere visible, such as the cash register or in your wallet (you can print them).

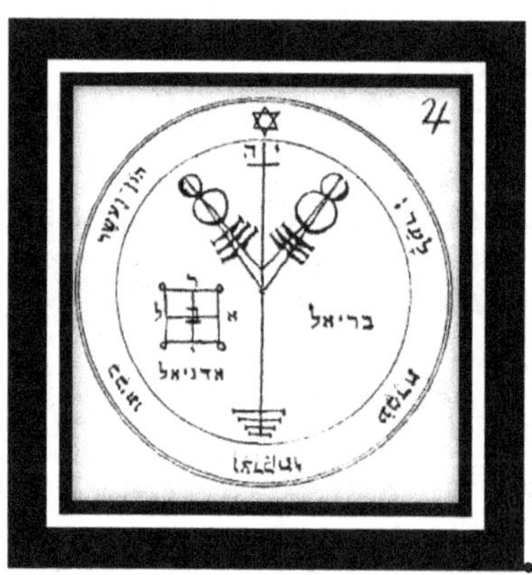

Affirmations to Receive Money

You should perform these decrees for 21 days so that you can see the results, if possible three times a day. If you repeat them out loud, they will be more powerful.

I have decided to live in opulence, I am an achiever.

I claim my share of wealth. I am prosperous. Money comes into my life in abundance and without any effort.

I am prosperous and rich, money flows in my life in a constant, permanent, and effortless way, money grows in my hands as trees grow in the field, everything I spend comes back to me multiplied, because I am the source of all wealth.

Vacations

Vacations provide physical and mental benefits. It has been proven that vacationing lowers stress levels and benefits the immune system. Sometimes planning a vacation causes stress because there are infinite options and deciding becomes a chimerical task.

Using astrology, understanding your personality provides insight into the ideal vacation spot for you.

***Aries**, an all-inclusive resort with outdoor sports activities in a warm location such as Punta Cana, Cancun and the Turks and Caicos Islands would be ideal. Australia is an exciting country that offers a wealth of emotions to make your heart race.*

***Taurus**, a stay in a luxurious resort on Cayman Island, or a luxurious vacation in Dubai, in a hotel that has all the amenities will be very appealing. Italy is a perfect country because there you will find everything you have always dreamed of love, charm, luxury, wonderful food, and first-class wines.*

***Gemini** loves to feel intellectually engaged. Travel with guided excursions such as a safari in Africa or researching the species of the Galapagos Islands offer the zodiac communicator a luxurious experience.*

Cancer, *short trips, surrounded by family and friends. Disney World, enjoying the attractions and its diverse foods is one option. In Orlando, Florida, there are multiple fantastic hotels and resorts, each with a unique and fascinating theme.*

Leo, *staying in a bungalow over the sea in Tahiti is fantastic for this sign. Another luxury alternative, something the lion loves, would be to rent a private tropical island in the Maldives, Fiji, or the Virgin Islands.*

Virgo, *Italy is your best option. This country will keep you well occupied. As an earth sign you connect with the world around you, places like La Romana in the Dominican Republic, Puerto Viejo in Costa Rica, and Belo Horizonte in Brazil will inject life into you.*

Libra, *go for cities with museums. Tropical vacations will not be as satisfying for Libra as touring the Louvre in Paris, the Acropolis Museum in Athens, Greece, the Prado Museum in Madrid, Spain or the Uffizi Gallery in Florence, Italy.*

Scorpion, *spend a few days on a secluded beach with liquor and massages. In Greece, Bali, St. Martin, or Hawaii you will find all these luxuries. Visiting heritage sites near your luxury hotel would be an extraordinary combination of tropical and cultural vacation. Mykonos and Roda in Greece are perfect destinations.*

Sagittarius, *explore the Camino de Santiago, a network of very different paths, all leading to the city of Santiago de Compostela. Each path has its history, heritage, and magic. Sagittarius is a traveler who craves new experiences so in Ireland you will find everything you are looking for.*

Capricorn, *a goal-oriented sign. Vacations where you can make new business relationships. China would be spectacular. Capricorn has a sense of historical value that other signs do not have, so countries like Israel and Egypt where history is present will make you feel at home.*

Aquarius *loves new ideas, unknown places, and new relationships. A fantastic country to visit would be Japan not only for its fascinating history and culture,* *but because each of its regions has something different to offer.*

Pisces, *a water sign that is happy with tropical vacations. A beachfront hotel would be ideal. The island "La Dique" in the Republic of Seychelles, perhaps the most beautiful beach in the world will be a sure success. Pisces, possessing a calm outlook on life, being ruled by Neptune makes you a creative thinker. Sweden is a country he should visit because there he will find a culture as innovative as he is.*

Who is your soul mate according to your zodiac sign?

When we hear the term "soul mates," we usually think of them as referring to members of a couple, i.e., someone with whom you have a strong sentimental-sexual connection. However, legitimate soul mates do not always relate to each other from that point of view, and often are not even interested in the sexual aspect of a relationship.

Your soul mate may not only be your partner, but also your parent, friend, child, grandparent, boss, or sister.

From the astrological point of view and considering that the lessons we need to learn before reaching the next spiritual level are the ones that define the type of affective relationships, we need to develop in life today, we can say that Cancer and Pisces are soul mates of Aries.

With Cancer and Pisces, Aries can not only focus better and resolve conflicts without violence, but also develop empathy, that is, the ability to put themselves in the other's place and learn to share.

These two signs do not like conflicts, and if they do arise, they prefer dialogue to any episode of brutality.

Aries can teach Cancer and Pisces not to need the approval of others, to be more risk-taking, and not to try to please everyone, i.e., to be more assertive.

The sensual Taurus, enemy of change, inbred relative of inertia, has as his soul mate Sagittarius and Gemini, two signs that know that life is a fascinating journey, but not a static one.

They can teach Taurus that it does not have to stay where it no longer must be for fear of uncertainty, and that there will always be certain situations or circumstances that will happen without us expecting them, and without us possessing any power to modify them. Taurus also has a lot to teach these signs.

Lessons of willpower, to have commitments with others, to be committed to what they do and to continue to the end with persistence, without haste or slowness. To have principles, and to be prudent.

Leo can balance a lot of karma with their soul mates belonging to Libra and Aquarius.

A Leo may become obstinate with a wrong idea or belief out of vanity; Libra and Aquarius know that behind an egocentric person there is a low self-esteem.

Libra will teach Leo equanimity and tolerance, to use reasoning and diplomacy to maintain smooth communication. Aquarius, the opposite sign to Leo, equipped with objective and fair judgment as they are never swayed by prejudice, will teach Leo to see people's hearts, to offer their shoulder and give sympathetic words in times of need.

Leo never hesitates when making decisions, and if they do, they do not manifest it, something that Libra should practice.

Fidelity is a hallmark in Leo, something unknown to Aquarius, and the little lions can give him moral lessons.

Virgo, known as perfectionists because of their immense fear of failure, has Scorpio and Capricorn as soul mates. Virgo likes to be rigorous in their decisions and has a prototype in almost every aspect of their life. This selectivity holds them back from following the movement of life.

Virgo will literally tear an entire project apart if they feel it wasn't perfect in the first place, something a Capricorn would never do as their vision will allow them to see that alternative measures can always be taken, without having to start over.

Capricorn is a sign sure of their own space, they don't make meaningless decisions, something Virgo sometimes does.

On the other hand, Scorpio can mitigate the worst and enhance the best of Virgo. Scorpio and Virgo have a practical approach to life; however, Scorpio is much more of a life-lover than Virgo. Scorpio will bring the decisiveness that Virgo lacks, and Virgo will bring control and rationality to the passionate Scorpio.

Virgo will make Capricorn more pleasant and playful at his side, isolating him from that excessive seriousness that he often shows in his face.

The madness

Madness has been revealed throughout history as an obscure, enigmatic, and conflicting truth. It has frightened us, we have ignored it and even accepted it, and as a result, the people who have supposedly suffered from it have been rejected, eliminated, and honored.

Any behavior that is incongruent with our reasoning is not necessarily an act of insanity, but a different way of proceeding.

It is a mistake if, when we feel affected or annoyed by the actions or follies of others, we banish them, since this does not make us more reasonable, balanced, or perfect, but rather makes us just as crazy.

Defining insanity is as complex as defining sanity, but all zodiac signs have their degree of insanity.

Cancer: They are temperamental. This causes them to have an incomprehensible personality seen from the outside. The popularity of crazy people was earned by their inconsistent character that sometimes disturbs the people around them.

Scorpio: They need change to be happy, they can do crazy things just to generate some action. For them having an outburst is normal because they are addicted to change and frenzies.

Pisces: *It is impossible for them not to infect you with their madness. Their instability and imbalance bother the people around them. They see everything as rosy, which makes them be called crazy because they are always floating on a cloud.*

Gemini: *He is famous for his duality. They are sometimes in conflict with themselves. They love challenges that involve danger. They love to plan impromptu adventures and are always ready to border the limits of maximum madness.*

Leo*: When the fire settles in their head, they think that everything that surrounds their life is more urgent than anything else. They are extravagant and have attitudes that for others are considered crazy. They can do things that a reasonable person would never do.*

Aries: *They upset themselves and anyone around them. They are stubborn and like to be the first in everything, even if for that they must commit crazy* *things. They do not know how to take it back, something that leads them to perform irrational acts.*

Aquarius: *A rebellious and free sign, which does not care in the least about the opinion they have of them. It acts in a capricious way, with crazy attitudes that break the paradigms.*

Sagittarius: *He is fun, but violent with his desire for action. They do not know how to measure the consequences of their actions, something that many consider madness. It is not strange to see them totally unbridled, crossing the terrain of irresponsibility.*

Libra: *They long for happiness and harmony, and to get it they are willing to do anything crazy. They are unstable, and that leads them to break their commitments, something that many consider crazy.*

Virgo: *They go to extremes and become obsessive. They have a vision of what they want written in stone, no one can give them advice, they do not let themselves be guided. When they do not listen, they commit various follies.*

Taurus*: When an idea lands in their mind there is no one to banish it, even committing crazy things to corroborate their hypothesis. Try to test their patience and you will discover how far their level of madness goes.*

Capricorn*: He forgets absolutely nothing, does not forgive and much less, forgets, if you do something wrong, do not worry because he will remind you for a lifetime to drive you completely crazy. Capricorn is insanely obsessive about control.*

The psychology behind the lottery.

Lottery games are very popular all over the world.

We all have the impossible dream of winning the lottery, since the illusion of being millionaires, by a stroke of luck, even if the odds are minimal, is the main reason why people play.

Players perceive that the cost of the lottery ticket, in relation to the profits they would obtain, if they win, is minuscule. We always perceive risk emotionally, and if it causes us pleasure, we tend to see the risk as insignificant and neutralize the emotion of danger, focusing only on the benefits.

Players see the lottery as a unique opportunity to be rewarded by investing little money, and with little exposure to risk.

Games have both traditional and superstitious aspects. Some people always play the same numbers because they are their favorites, relate them to a significant date, or have dreamed them.

Others play at a specific time, day, or place. When we think we are in control, we feel confident, because when we choose the numbers ourselves, instead of playing at random, although the chances of being right are the same, we have the impression that we are controlling destiny, and that the chances are in our favor.

There are people who only play for fun, in these cases the lottery transcends the economic cost, becoming a fun that is enlivened when they conjecture everything, they can do with the money they would acquire.

There are five psychological descriptions of individual lottery players:

The adventurer, *who is bewitched by games involving large sums of money, speculating with random numbers, and with planned numbers.*

The competitor, *who insists on showing off through gambling that he bets to win.*

The greedy, *who has no boundaries for gambling, and is not afraid to take risks when betting.*

The tactician, *never playing risky, looks for tactics, strategies, and numerical sets when playing the numbers.*

The superstitious person, *who always plays the same number combinations, uses talismans, rituals, or will buy his tickets on a specific date and place.*

Is there a trick or formula to win the lottery?

That question is still unanswered. There are many who speculate, and claim, that you are more likely to be struck by lightning before you win the lottery. Although others study the possibilities with great perseverance and subtlety.

Playing the lottery, or any other game of chance if it is done with measure, is a cheap way to buy illusions and confidence in the future. The complication arises when the person does not control his impulses to play, generating an addiction to gambling and falling into compulsive gambling.

A gambling addict is an individual to whom gambling causes great difficulties at work and in his family relationships, since losses induce him to gamble larger amounts of money with the aspiration of recovering the lost money. This becomes a vicious circle, and the only way to solve it is with psychotherapeutic treatment.

The best gift for zodiac signs.

Gift giving is a universal way to show that we care and appreciate a person, but gift buying can be a challenge, for some a real headache.

The planets can help you once, knowing the zodiac sign of the person, you may be able to make the ideal gift.

***Fire signs: Aries, Leo and Sagittarius** like gifts that make them feel important, related to sports, travel, and technology.*

A professional digital camera, the latest model of iPhone, a plane ticket with hotel included to an exotic tourist spot or with historical background, business books, sportswear or exercise equipment, lottery tickets, bottles of fine wine and exclusive branded shoes will please these signs greatly.

***Taurus, Virgo and Capricorn**, who belong to the earth element, are sometimes traditional, but that doesn't mean they don't like gifts from recognized brands.*

A painting of a famous painter, a belt or briefcase to carry their work papers, a wallet with their initials, branded perfumes, massages or body treatments, a pet, bathrobes, cozy pajamas, or even aromatherapy diffusers will make them happy.

Air signs: Gemini, Libra and Aquarius *are not materialistic, and the functionality of a gift is much more important than the price. Their imagination is abundant, and anything that stimulates this capacity appeals to them.*

A cell phone, computer or IPad, books on personal growth, spirituality, philosophy and alternative therapies, self-help and economic empowerment courses, a telescope, tickets to the opera or theater, an animal that does not have to be caged, quartz, essential oils, incense, and after-bath colognes will be highly appreciated by these signs.

Cancer, Scorpio and Pisces*, the water signs, will love personalized gifts. Cooking utensils, a romantic dinner on the beach under the moonlight, a relaxing massage in a spa, daring lingerie, slippers or a comfortable sofa to watch TV, a bottle of champagne, scented candles, amulets, astrology books, a set of tarot cards, lotions, perfumes and beauty accessories, wine, cookies, preserves and all variety of gourmet products are on the list of gifts that these signs will accept with great pleasure.*

Giving gifts is a blessing, it is a gesture of generosity; giving gifts is a symbolic act that represents a compliment, an attention to someone we want to please and symbolizes the affection we profess.

When we give gifts, relationships are improved and strengthened, and joy is generated.

The zodiac signs and their fears.

The twelve signs of the zodiac symbolize twelve essential archetypes of the human personality, but at the same time they are psychological prototypes, which is why each of the zodiac signs has a very specific and personal fear.

Let us remember that fear is an essential human alarm and defense mechanism. It only becomes a problem when it is excessive.

*Fears are insecurities and sometimes we project them with the opposite actions as is the case of the **Aries** sign; recognized for their iron will, nothing and nobody paralyzes them. They love to control everything, and their most ingrained fear is to fail or ask for help, because for them this is synonymous of weakness.*

***Taurus** is the most stubborn of the earth signs. Change terrifies them, as well as running out of money, they spend their lives saving because poverty frightens them.*

***Gemini**, the communicator of the zodiac, a bit anxious and insecure, they try to attract attention because they dread looking boring. Legitimate children of the*

Moon, Cancers love their safety zone because no one can hurt them there, they are terrified of loneliness and rejection.

__Leo__, the king of the zodiac, leaders and brave, were not born to lose. Their most ingrained fear is to go unnoticed; they prefer to be spoken ill of, but not to be ignored.

The master of neatness __Virgo__ sometimes becomes compulsive about health, so they are hypochondriacs. Their main fear is getting sick, but disorganization scares them more than anything else.

Exceptionally intelligent __Libra__ are indecisive and therein lies their primary fear: making decisions. Another of their fears is loneliness.

The enigmatic and seductive __Scorpios__ have an elephant's memory, they fear betrayal and if you do something they dislike, they will keep it from you forever. Never keep a secret from a Scorpio.

The adventurer of the zodiac, __Sagittarius__ panics about commitment because the demands are terrifying. They are very funny, but behind that smile hides the fear of being deceived.

*Demanding to the extreme, **Capricorns** never stray from their goals; their main fear is to make mistakes, especially at the professional level. They are self-sacrificing and fear not achieving their dreams.*

*The rebellious and utopian **Aquarius** fear losing their freedom, this would mean losing their own essence. They always have many friendships, but none of them bind them. They need the group, but do not want the group to need them.*

*Peace is synonymous with **Pisces**, they hate confrontations. Compassionate to the core, they are afraid to see others suffer. They are a little insecure, have stage fright and fear rejection.*

Some old astrology books hold Saturn totally responsible for fear in a natal chart, I think that for fear to originate, the alliance of several planets with their corresponding energies must manifest.

That is, fears are represented by several planets linked by aspects, there is no specific planet that is necessarily related to the development of any type of fear.

Moon in the Sign of Cancer

Cancer is the most emotional sign of the zodiac, as it functions at the level of feelings and emotions.

The Moon rules the sign of Cancer, which means that the Moon in this sign could openly express and explore all emotions. Sometimes people with the Moon in Cancer are slaves to their emotions and struggle to keep them under control.

If your Moon is in the sign of Cancer, emotional connections are very important to you. In fact, you need to have emotional connections with other people to survive.

The bonds you share are what help you remember that you are not alone, and that desire for emotional support means you long to feel part of a whole.

However, you must remember to take care of your own needs, otherwise you may become dependent on the emotional support of others.

The Moon in Cancer possesses a strong maternal instinct, and makes you feel secure when you know that the people you love are protected.

When you do not connect emotionally with others you interpret this as your emotional needs not being met, something you really need to survive. If this happens your soul would go into a state of terror, because you cannot really subsist if you do not meet those needs. Your darkest fear is to be alone in the world.

The person with the Moon in Cancer when he feels threatened, his reaction is to hide and try to reestablish his emotional connections.

Safety and security are most important to Cancer, so habits and routine are comforting to these people. The more secure their surroundings are, the more secure they will feel.

In romantic relationships, they feel more secure when they have a deep connection with their partner, and need to believe that their partner will take their feelings into consideration.

When you recognize that you can meet your own survival needs without the support of others, you will be able to create better emotional connections with the people in your life.

You should be aware of your expectations and desires for emotional support.

The importance of the Ascendant Sign

The Sun sign has a major impact on who we are, but the Ascendant is what really defines us, and that could even be the reason why you don't identify with some traits of your zodiac sign.

Really the energy that your sun sign gives you makes you feel different from the rest of the people, for that reason, when you read your horoscope sometimes you feel identified and gives sense to some predictions, and that happens because it helps you to understand how you could feel and what will happen to you, but it only shows you a percentage of what could really be.

The Ascendant is different from the Sun sign because it reflects who we are superficially, that is, how others see you or the energy you transmit to people, and this is so real that you may meet someone and if you predict their sign, you may have discovered their Ascendant sign and not their Sun sign.

In summary, the characteristics you see in someone when you first meet them is the Ascendant, but since our lives are affected by the way we relate to others, the Ascendant has a major impact on our daily lives.

It is a bit complex to explain how the Ascendant sign is calculated or determined, because it is not the position of a planet that determines it, but the sign that was rising on the eastern horizon at the time of your birth, as opposed to your sun sign, which depends on the precise time you were born.

Thanks to technology and the Universe today is easier than ever to know this information, of course if you know your birth time, or if you have an idea of the time but there is not a margin of more than hours, because there are many websites that make the calculation by entering the data, astro.com is one of them, but there is infinite.

This way, when you read your horoscope you can also read your Ascendant and know more personalized details, you are going to see that from now on if you do this your way of reading the horoscope will change and you will know why that Sagittarius is so modest and pessimistic if in reality they are so exaggerated and optimistic, and this is perhaps because he has a Capricorn Ascendant, or because that Scorpio colleague is always talking about everything, no doubt he has a Gemini Ascendant.

I am going to synthesize the characteristics of the different Ascendants, but this is also very general since these characteristics are modified by planets in conjunction with the Ascendant, planets aspecting the Ascendant, and the position of the ruler planet of the sign in the Ascendant.

For example, a person with an Ascendant in Sagittarius with its ruling planet, Jupiter, in Aries will respond to the environment a little differently than another person, also with an Ascendant in Sagittarius, but with Jupiter in Scorpio.

Similarly, a person with a Pisces Ascendant who has Saturn conjunct him will "behave" differently than someone with a Pisces Ascendant who does not have that aspect.

All these factors modify the Ascendant, astrology is very complex, and horoscopes are not read or made with tarot cards, because astrology is not only an art but also a science.

It can be common to confuse these two practices, and this is because, although they are two totally different concepts, they have some points in common. One of these common points is based on their origin and is that both procedures have been known since ancient times.

They are also similar in the symbols they use, since both present ambiguous symbols that need to be interpreted, requiring specialized reading and training to know how to interpret these symbols.

There are thousands of differences, but one of the main ones is that while in tarot the symbols are perfectly understandable at first glance, being figurative cards, although it is necessary to know how to interpret them well, in astrology we observe an abstract system which is necessary to know previously to interpret them, and of course it must be said that, although we can recognize the tarot cards, anyone can not interpret them correctly.

Interpretation is also a difference between the two disciplines because while tarot does not have an exact time reference, since the cards are placed in time only thanks to the questions asked in the corresponding spread, astrology does refer to a specific position of the planets in history, and the interpretation systems used by both are diametrically opposed.

The astrological chart is the basis of astrology, and the most important aspect to make the prediction. The astrological chart must be perfectly elaborated for the reading to be successful and to learn more about the person.

To draw up a birth chart, it is necessary to know all the data about the birth of the person in question.

It must be known exactly, from the exact time it was delivered, to the place where it was done.

The position of the planets at the time of birth will reveal to the astrologer the points he needs to draw up the birth chart.

Astrology is not only about knowing your future, but also about knowing the important points of your existence, both present and past, to make better decisions to decide your future.

Astrology will help you to know yourself better, so that you can change the things that block you or enhance your qualities.

And if the astrological chart is the basis of astrology, the tarot reading is fundamental in the latter discipline. Like who makes you the astrological chart, the seer who makes you the tarot spread, will be the key to the success of your reading, so it is best to ask for tarot readers recommended, and although surely you cannot answer specifically to all the questions you ask yourself in your life, a correct reading of the tarot spread, and the cards that come out in the roll, will help guide you about the decisions you make in your life.

In summary, astrology, and tarot use symbolism, but the main question is how all this symbolism is interpreted.

truly a person who masters both techniques will undoubtedly be a great help to the people who will ask for advice.

Many astrologers combine both disciplines, and regular practice has taught me that both usually flow very well, providing an enriching component in all prediction issues, but they are not the same and you cannot do a horoscope with tarot cards, nor can you do a tarot reading with an astrological chart.

Ascendant in Cancer

People with this Ascendant avoid conflict whenever possible. These people must learn to understand their own rhythms since they cling to their feelings and do not give them up until another stronger feeling appears.

Emotions and the search for security are most important for people with this Ascendant.

An Ascendant in Cancer who tries to find themselves in other people will absorb the negative emotions of the other. Being so empathetic to others, they may think that the negative feelings they perceive are their own.

It is necessary that this Ascendant learns to distinguish well where these emotions come from so that they do not remain stuck in the memories of the past.

The empathy of this Ascendant allows them to have an excellent perception of their surroundings, but their objective will always be to seek a relationship that offers them security and stability.

Aries - Cancer Ascendant

This zodiacal combination clashes with each other, given the strong Aries energy and the Cancer sign's tendency to avoid conflict. These people's lives can be subject to constant change.

They enjoy participating in social events and sharing with friends and family.

In the labor area, they are focused and do their best to succeed and consolidate their projects. Regardless of their profession, if they set their minds to it, they will be able to achieve whatever they set their minds to.

In love, they put their dignity above all else and this can cause conflicts. Although they are always very generous, empathetic, and protective.

People with Ascendant in Cancer are influenced by their family and can be manipulated by them.

Taurus - Cancer Ascendant

This astral combination values their friendships, considering them as part of their family. They are supportive and empathetic individuals.

At work, they succeed thanks to their friendly and empathetic charisma, as they know how to treat people well and are always rewarded for their character.

In love, although their feelings are strong, they value freedom and trust. These will be key emotions to preserve their relationships. However, sometimes they can make wrong decisions.

Emotions and sensitivity are the greatest difficulties for these people as they can cause psychosomatic problems.

Gemini - Cancer Ascendant

Gemini with Cancer Ascendant are people with great communication skills.

For these people, the most important thing is to find a job where they can develop their creativity and feel comfortable with what they are doing, and who they are connecting with.

Occasionally, a lack of self-esteem may not allow them to develop their full potential.

In general, they are much more sensitive and empathetic, but in love, feeling secure and valued is a primordial need.

Some hide in the face of any conflict, as the fear of being exposed terrifies them.

Cancer - Cancer Ascendant

This combination of signs reinforces the characteristics of Cancer. They are the most affectionate and protective people of the zodiac.

Cancer with Cancer Ascendant lives their emotions intensely and this allows them to be extremely perceptive to the emotions of others.

In the area of work, they are not very competitive. They always try to find a comfortable position in which they do not have to work hard, but which allows them to live without worries.

In their sentimental relationships they are prone to idealize their partner, alienating themselves from reality. They usually give in without thinking twice to the desires of the one they love. Sometimes they are unstable and have no emotional control in their lives.

Leo - Cancer Ascendant

Leo with Cancer Ascendant are very protective people, they love luxuries, but they love to share them with those who belong to their closest circle. For these people their loved ones are the priority in their lives, and they like to shower them with gifts.

For this Ascendant it is a priority to have financial stability because it offers them a lot of security.

Having access to financial resources guarantees that they can live the way they want to live. They strive to find ways to be financially prosperous.

In the work area, they love to acquire new knowledge and start projects, as they are enterprising people with a great fighting spirit.

In love they can be very jealous and manipulative with their partner.

Some use social status and material possessions as gauges to value people, appreciating only appearances.

Virgo - Cancer Ascendant
Virgo with Cancer Ascendant are people who have a great ability to communicate, and an incredible imagination and intelligence.

They possess extraordinary social skills since they are interested in having many relationships and are also very pleasant to deal with.

In love they focus on family; this is the perfect type of person to build a solid family.

They are sometimes shy, but when you get to know them, they are charming.

Libra - Cancer Ascendant

Libra with Cancer Ascendant is a union of affectionate and expressive signs. This combination is always successful, especially in relationships.

These people will always be looking for stability, and to form a home.

With the rest of the relationships, they are balanced people and know how to bring order and be mediators if necessary.

Occasionally they like to play the role of victims, projecting their mistakes.

Scorpio - Cancer Ascendant

his union of two signs of the water element reinforces the typical characteristics of the element. The sensitivity of this combination is outstanding.

These individuals must reflect and analyze each opportunity so that they can truly discern what is in their best interest.

In the labor area, they may not advance as they would like to, since they sometimes tend to be pessimistic.

The way they give affection is related to their artistic interests. In their relationships they regularly do not limit themselves with their partner but become very permissive.

They may confuse passion with love, and maintaining a stable relationship can be difficult for them.

Sagittarius - Cancer Ascendant

Sagittarius with Cancer Ascendant are super intuitive people, but with outstanding faculties for practical work. They are confident in their abilities to do any job.

They are very focused and sensible, and like to share with their family. However, the desire to be accepted and loved pushes them to make wrong decisions.

They can become so committed to their work that it can even be detrimental to their health and relationships. They love to reproach others even when they always make the same mistakes.

Capricorn - Ascendant Cancer

This zodiacal combination complements each other. Cancer's sensitivity coupled with Capricorn's discipline results in dutiful people who value commitments.

In love they prefer to share their life with someone they can trust. They are very responsible and honest individuals who seek the same in a relationship.

At work, they are involved in many projects at the same time, but they are independent and reliable.

There is a tendency for these people to stay in a relationship that should end due to lack of affection, since maintaining it by tradition seems to them to be the right thing to do.

Aquarius - Cancer Ascendant

People with this influence are protective to the extreme. Sometimes they tend to be unbalanced, because sometimes they are driven by reason rather than by intuition.

In the work area, they are always successful, especially in government-related jobs.

In love they love to maintain their independence, but when they fall in love, they give everything for their partner.

A negative aspect of this Ascendant is that sometimes they are influenced by other people.

Pisces - Cancer Ascendant

Pisces with Cancer Ascendant is extremely sensitive, and dreamy. They love novelty and are focused on constantly learning.

In the labor area, they are ambitious and fighters since they seek success and never give up until they obtain it.

Love is important to them and sharing moments with their family is essential, although they are lovesick.

Bibliography

Some information was extracted from the books published by the authors: Love for all Hearts, Money for all Pockets and Horoscope 2022 and 2024.

Articles written in the Nuevo Herald by one of the writers.

About the Authors

In addition to her astrological knowledge, Alina A. Rubi has an abundant professional education; she holds certifications in Psychology, Hypnosis, Reiki, Bioenergetic Crystal Healing, Angelic Healing, Dream Interpretation and is a Spiritual Instructor. Rubi has knowledge of Gemology, which she uses to program stones or minerals and turn them into powerful Amulets or Talismans of protection.

Rubi has a practical and results-oriented character, which has allowed her to have a special and integrative vision of several worlds, facilitating solutions to specific problems. Alina writes the Monthly Horoscopes for the website of the American Association of Astrologers; you can read them at www.astrologers.com. At this moment she writes a weekly column in the newspaper El Nuevo Herald on spiritual topics, published every Sunday in digital form and on Mondays in print. He also has a program and weekly Horoscope on the YouTube channel of this newspaper. Her Astrological Yearbook is published every year in the newspaper "Diario las Américas", under the column Rubi Astrologa.

Rubi has written several articles on astrology for the monthly publication "Today's Astrologer", has taught classes on Astrology, Tarot, Palm Reading, Crystal Healing, and Esotericism. She has weekly videos on esoteric topics on her YouTube channel: Rubi Astrologa. She had her own Astrology show broadcasted daily through Flamingo T.V., has been interviewed by several T.V. and radio programs, and every year she publishes her "Astrological Yearbook" with the horoscope sign by sign, and other interesting mystical topics.

She is the author of the books "Rice and Beans for the Soul" Part I, II, and III, a compilation of esoteric articles, published in English, Spanish, French, Italian and Portuguese. "Money for All Pockets", "Love for All Hearts", "Health for All Bodies", Astrological Yearbook 2021, Horoscope 2022, Rituals and Spells for Success in 2022, Spells and Secrets, Astrology Classes, Rituals and Charms 2024 and Chinese Horoscope 2024 are all available in five languages: English, Italian, French, Japanese and German.

Rubi speaks English and Spanish perfectly, combining all her talents and knowledge in her readings. She currently resides in Miami, Florida.

*For more information you can visit **the website** www.esoterismomagia.com*

Alina A. Rubi is the daughter of Alina Rubi. She is currently studying psychology at Florida International University.

Since she was a child, she has been interested in all metaphysical and esoteric subjects and has practiced astrology and Kabbalah since she was four years old. She has knowledge of Tarot, Reiki, and Gemology. She is not only the author, but also the editor, along with her sister Angeline A. Rubi, of all the books published by her and her mother.

*For more information, please contact her by email: **rubiediciones29@gmail.com***